REFLECTIONS

Daily Thoughts and Prayers

Volume 2

For further contact and information: https://www.rkmireland.org/contact_us

Volume 2 first edited and printed: May 2022.

FOREWORD

During the Covid pandemic Swami Purnananda, the Spiritual Director of the Ramakrishna Vedanta Centre in Dublin, and an Advaita Vedanta monk, started writing short poems followed by a short Prayer, which he posted on the Internet. The poems were his reflections on everyday events, on the ideas of spiritual leaders of the past, on the nature of Maya, on works of art, on places, animals, science, technology, in short, on all aspects of life experienced. Each thought had a beautiful accompanying photograph. In these reflections Swami Purnananda's aim was to suggests that all of our life experience can be viewed as lessons that reveal the truth that we and all existence are One: the supreme message of Vedanta. The bleak atmosphere during this period could then be viewed differently. The Vedanta message of Unity is very powerful. It is a message for all humanity and is expressed as an eternal law that underpins existence.

As a theoretical physicist I am attracted to this profound vision of Unity offered by Advaita Vedanta and would like to take this opportunity to explain one scientist's take on the Vedanta. The Vedanta vision comes from answering the question: "What is Real?" We need a definition. The sages tell us that Reality must be permanent and unchanging. It must thus be outside the limitations of space-time-causality, where change is the norm; but the world experienced constantly changes and is thus according to the definition not Real. It is an illusion: it is Maya. Is there anything we know that is Real? It seems to be an impossible definition. Why did the sages introduce this idea and why is the idea important? We are, reassured by the sages and told "Do not worry. Reality defined does exist. You can directly experience this Reality because you are this Reality. The idea is important because it reveals your true nature." This stunning but puzzling statement is followed by an explanation that tells us that this deep truth about our true nature is hidden from us but that we can realize it if we seek it and that every night during deep sleep we all experience the grand unity of existence. During deep sleep all differences disappear. The sages then tell us that there are different paths that can be followed to reach the goal of self-realization but that all the paths are difficult. Guidance from a Guru is recommended. The many paths, however, converge when there is self-realization. Then one directly experiences the unchanging Reality that underpins existence and one understands that the world experienced is an illusion and one understands ones true nature. We then directly know that we are all One, that we have great capabilities and we are linked together with all of existence. This uplifting message was shouted out by Swami Vivekananda to all humanity: Arise and discover your True nature. Once we realize our true nature we are transformed. Theoretical physics and the biological sciences also suggest that the world seen is an illusion: underlying the observed material world, physics tells us that there is an unseen world of energy, waves, chance and constant change

3

controlled by the dance of electrons but these changes obey unchanging laws. The material world experienced is a construct. For human beings too we now know that what we see, feel, smell or touch are all constructs. The light image picked up by the eye, or the sound waves picked by our ears or the smell picked by our nose or the touch sensation picked by our skin, are all converted to electric signals written in the brain's own abstract code. This code is processed by the brain to give us an integrated constructed picture of the world. It is a construct: an illusion! Furthermore individual vision or other sensory signals cannot be distinguished from each other from their representations as electric signals. All sensory signals look the same. There is thus a unity in the nature of the representations of sensory signals. But they lead to different experiences. The differences of experiences, come from the different dedicated circuits used to carry different sensory signals. Thus our experiences are not Real. They are brain constructs. In the field of brain science, however, no unchanging laws that underly events observed have been found as yet. Moving on to the scale of different types of living creatures we note that advances made in the genetics tell us that all lifeforms have an underlying universal common building code. While all non-life forms, studied in physics, can be constructed from a simpler building code. However both the living and the non-living world hide a profound underlying unity in the sense that they both obey the unchanging laws of physics and chemistry. These results of science thus resonate with the insights of Vedanta: the illusory nature of the experienced world is now established by science, the convergence to a unity of description is emerging and the presence of unchanging Reality in the form of unchanging laws of nature have been found. The Vedantic vision of Reality also suggests that seekers of knowledge should find universal laws underly their special field of investigation. Thus it is expected that unchanging laws, not known at present, will emerge in brain science. However the Vedantic vision is much stronger than the vision of unity uncovered by Science. Vedanta suggests that the underlying Unity behind existence is one. This insight is missing from science and is likely to remain missing, since in science objects are differentiated even in the unchanging laws formulated. Thus science by its nature can approach but can never capture the full majesty of Reality suggested in Vedanta.

In Swami Purnananda's book the uplifting message of Vedantic unity is present in all of his reflections, sometimes explicitly, sometimes hidden in parables or stories and sometimes whispered through images. Perhaps reading and looking at the beautiful photographs then will help those who face stress and uncertainty in their lives.

Prof Siddhartha Sen, Sc.D (MIT)

Emeritus Fellow, Trinity College Dublin; Member of the Royal Irish Academy

PREFACE

Since this is the second volume of "Reflections", I repeat much of the preface in Volume 1. This volume continues to offer a collection of daily thoughts in the form of poems and matching prayers and photographs. These correspond to a second of 4 volumes spanning the 365 days of the year. The offerings have been re-edited, and they were daily from ideas that came in the early mornings. They were written with a 'let go" attitude of a recipient of divine grace that was sure to flow.

The carefully selected photographs and pictures were for the most part supplied by a keen photographer, who in a spirit of service and humility wished to remain anonymous, but he served as my collaborator and encouraged me over the year.

As mentioned previously, these presentations have been structured around a principle that if we can shift our thinking in a nobler way, we can systematically deal with any physical, emotional, and spiritual difficulty. For this reason, the daily "thoughts and prayers" are really Reflections on teachings of wiser inspired people who are attuned to the eternal and universal truths encapsulated in the Vedanta philosophy. Hence the title of this book is "Reflections". For this reason, my hope is that readers will truly reflect of the sometimes-subtle messages that will take the reader on a meditative journey to a deeper level where there may be a flash of understanding that inspires. I have tried to share with the reader the way that I learned to adopt the sporting attitude to life that I found so useful in practical life.

I repeat what I stated in the Volume 1 preface that "I am aware of my own literary limitations in writing these Reflections and the mixed style they are written in. I am blissfully ignorant of what constitutes a well written poem or not. Some are in rhyming metre and others more in prose and still others a combination of the two, but it is my hope that they will serve their purpose of uplifting spirits and pacifying the unsettled mind."

My deep indebtedness goes to devotees who received the writings with such enthusiasm and particularly to Dr Georgiana Ifrim, who is Associate Professor at the School of Computer Science, University College Dublin. She untiringly undertook to format and publish this work with the resolve "I will not rest until I have this book in my hands." My thanks also goes to her husband Deepak Ajwani who faithfully, uploaded these thoughts & prayers onto my Blog page. Last but not least, my thanks to the very learned Professor Siddhartha Sen who gracefully wrote such a wonderful and supportive foreword to this Volume.

Swami Purnananda

Introduction

Since this Volume is part of an overall four volume work, Volume 1's introduction really serves as the best introduction for this and subsequent volumes. There I mentioned that "Reflections" was suggestive of reflected images on water, or mirroring of opinions, or thoughtfulness such as "Is the perceived world merely reflections caused by subtle quantum ripples on a blissful ocean base?", "Is the fleeting world as substantial as we deem it to be?", "What is the underlying reality that is a life-giver?". This Book in its overall four volumes matches all of these and provides another religio-philosophical dimension that we and all existence are reflections of a single entity.

There is a universality about human experiences of struggle, tragedy that has been emphasised more as contemporary life provides more detailed multi-sensory information to our senses on a daily basis. It seems to me that the remedy for the resultant deleterious psychological effects on the recipients is to use our inherent capacity to shift our attention to higher and nobler insights. These can be derived from better observations that incorporate the necessary shift to the fullness of our own subjective Consciousness.

As in Volume 1, this volume contains verses and prayers that are constructed to elevate a mood and provoke meaningful thought as well as provide a heartfelt opportunity to express something of wonder, adoration, and thankfulness. For those who have been reading these collections on modern media daily have found that if they begin their day with these reflections the themes tend to resonate throughout the whole day, elevate the mind and delight them.

It is true that the themes are grounded in universal philosophy and are often mystical in their nature, but they suggest that the answers and methods are fully within us if we only seek them out with a kind of bold thrill. As mentioned in Volume 1, "problems and conflicts have matching creative solutions deep within us. Sometimes the content is puzzling, requiring the unravelling of the subtlety, others reflect a humour that promotes a certain positive position, but all are mirrored reflections of previously thought of ideas".

"The prayers are non-sectarian, heartfelt, and personal and so may be by-passed by the more cerebrally inclined, but those who have read them, reflected on them, echoed them and absorbed them, sometimes find them more poignant and rewarding than the Thoughts themselves. Seen through eyes of wonder, the world explained by science has an aesthetic beauty that a non-seeing eye misses. When we re-examine what is in front more diligently, we find a world of wonder that elevates the soul, as it were. If we were able to play a discerning game that sees through to the very heart of things, our lives would be transformed completely. We would have discovered fulfilment and a peace and harmony that collectively could transform the seemingly troubled world. "

For those picking up this Volume for the first time and who find great value in it and who are not acquainted with the first volume, I encourage them to complete the cycle of thought contained for completeness' sake.

May Love and Blessings be with all beings on their pilgrim journey.

Swami Purnananda

Thought

Let our solemn thoughts align
Reflections and resolve combine
On one who taught and suffered
Corporeal pain for us offered

Each one has their cross to bear
Forbearance shown by Saviour
Let us accept with cheerful gait
Whatever is our self-formed fate

Cross out self-image of the "I"
Egocentric views defy
What greater love than to die
For another's freedom to buy

Reviewing lessons from the past
Corrections now made to last
With anguish, trials, austerities
Play life's game with skillful ease
Next scene dawns a glorious day
When rising sun rays blaze away

Prayer

O sweet sacrifice let me feel Thy presence now as I sit at thy holy feet marveling at Thy love marked in blood. May I learn to carry my small crosses with forbearance and fully follow Thy every guided step.

Thought

Be alert as thoughts stream in
Aware of every passing sin.
Burn mind's lamp night and day
Keep vigil as you watch and pray

When the Lord appears disguised
Be sure that He is recognised
And mindful of your own demise
Keep vigil in each enterprise

Each life is like a candle flame
Oblivious of from whence it came
Lit and fueled till wind snuffs out
Keep vigil to know what it's about

As soul's darkness fades to grey
And leading light announces day
Keenly watch that silent hour
Keep vigil over kingdom's power

Prayer

O Leading Light fix my mind on thee that my attention may not stray. Lead me out of the darkness of the desert to the light of thy kingdom. Fix my heart on thine as yours is fixed on me. You move these limbs of this earth car for thy glory alone.

Thought

Cheerful chirping songs of praise
Greet growing glowing solar rays
Shy red orb over blankets peep
Stirring earth from restful sleep

Fully dressed bursts forth in gold
With generous arms a thousand-fold
Fire whirl and dance in fused array
Proclaimed by earth as glorious day

This shining celestial radiant face
That eclipses every darkened place
Is lit and stoked from deep within
By self-lit Lord royally enthroned

One who ignites the cosmic fire
Surrounded by an angels' choir
That raises energy and breath
Is ruler over life and death

The Cosmic Egg, the Surya Lord
All tell of Birth and Logos Word
Elation felt in well found creed
The Lord is risen - He is risen indeed!

Prayer

O Lord let me always feel the rising breathless elation of Thy tangible breath; please always reveal Thy Glory to me in the symbols of nature, where by your grace we romp and play. Let us meditate on the glory of that Being who has produced this universe; may He enlighten our minds.

DAY 4

Thought

For hope of change and cool relief
In lofty heights of strong belief
Many miles - course travelling
Finding us again at the beginning

Some days we see the mountains clear
A distant view makes them seem near
Sometimes the mists come in to hide
And mountain shapes to eyes denied

God's vision comes in this same way
When our attention does not stray
To those who access Divine Grace
The yearning heart will see His face

Prayer

Dearest Lord, closer than breathing, remove the mist from my eyes so that they may be ever fixed on Thee. May I be satisfied with small steps and precious revelations and be thankful for the journey.

DAY 5

Thought

Jagged shapes breaking sky
Glass and steel rising high
Wisdom says that space remains
Not carved or spoiled by shadow stains

Fragmented pixels on a screen
Do not divide wholistic scene
Dividedness and change are due
To our limited mistaken view

So too that One has made it seem
That It sports in waking dream
But really there is naught to fear
Since no one else but One is here

Prayer

O Lord, your Divine hand is always raised in assurance. Let us feel the seamless oneness of your being so that all our fears dissolve and are replaced in the warmth and bliss of your unity.

Thought

Fearful forest dwelling beasts
Alert to all the dangers round
Protect, preserve home and life
As senses scan the sky and floor
The rustled leaf and crack of twig
Shifts the ready attention easily

No different in our daily life
Same instincts duly tend to rule
Along with coffee, news and job
With a homely mortgaged nest
Preserve competing in the herd
Alert still to the dangers heard

Sounds come to ears in waves unseen
So used are we to soft and loud
But when within deep silence reigns
And calmness finds its real home
There is the still sweet voice of God
That lifts the body mind and soul

Prayer
Lord, let me sit in your presence, a mere child; Let me allow your presence and grace to bathe me in stillness; stillness of body and stillness of mind that is your very throne room. Let the peace that passes all understanding pervade.

Thought

Seekers ask, "Lord where art Thou?"
But He replies "You see me not?
My voice is heard in whispering leaves
My face shines forth on rippling waves

My breath is felt upon your skin
My joy is sent through warbling birds
I blink as every heavenly star
That guards and makes your destiny

Look up and see my skin of space
Look down and feel my lap of earth
I am soft grass grown at your feet
Your body warmth is my heartbeat

So, look for Me where 'ere you be
My child your guiding Light is Me"

Prayer

Lord open my eyes that I might feel thy presence in, through as and beyond all things. Blessed Inner Controller and Divine Helmsman, thanks and praise to Thee for carrying me to the distant shore. Ever keep my heart in yours.

DAY 8

Thought

Trees hold close some secrets rare
Knowing stories past unknown
Of how vast branches reaching up
Have come from subtle essences

In hidden worlds in soil confined
Whispered wonders are combined
Subtly inwardly urging forth
Unfolding from the womb of earth

Young sapling sprouts from tiny seed
Multiple cells with knowledge packed
That we might see Its force irresistibly
Revealed as glorious energy

Prayer

O Lord subtly present and ready for when I get tired of playing. Thou art my eye of eye and mind of mind. May my eyes see thee and my mind know thee. From thy unfolding presence, reveal to me thy totality.

Thought

Ancient ones took note of time
To synchronise events to chime
With nature's writhe and dance
Welcoming auspicious chance
To neutralise society's wrongs
With festivals, chants and songs

As the moon and seasons played
Prayers to deities would cascade
For those presiding over rain
Ensured abundant harvest grain

Students too were taught to move
Thought currents helpful to improve
To tune thought currents happily
With steadily directed energy
Brings to the unsettled stability
In the world at large and locally
Generous thought devoid of pique
Transforms each day, month and week

Prayer

O Lord of time, you offer endless opportunities to worship Thee; grant that I may not squander these with distractions wherein my love for Thee strays. Thy current of thought is always flowing, grant that I may steer it usefully.

Thought
From age to age in Cosmic Time
Clash and crash and slash and burn
Violent forces try their best
To win a war of opposites

From age-to-age dramatic scenes
Played out in worldly stage well set
Sees evil gain the upper hand
And reign throughout the cosmic land

Light of truth and goodness wins
With victory's foot upon the head
Restoring Peace and Harmony
Both overall and in man's realm

What weapons can be used for us?
What gift to glean from such a scene?
Inner strength of will we find
To rout the enemies of mind

Discrimination is our sword
And arrows too our skill in thought
A fortress held with strength as mace
Dispensed through protective Grace

Prayer

O Lord, may I daily feel thy secure presence in moments when I feel I am banished, abandoned and alone. Grant me the strength to control the mind on the one hand and surrender to Thee on the other.

Thought

Children may ask why trees are small
At distances beyond them all?
And skip about in spellbound cheer
To clamber on same branches near

Are we not too mere simple youths?
Who cannot see the things we choose?
In journeys shown by lines of trees
Our vision shifts to things that please

When mystic path becomes our way
To search out for safe place to stay
With each step inner thrills revealed
And precious Self no more concealed

Prayer

Lord, ever hold my hand as we delightfully explore the inner and outer worlds together;
grant that I may, with wonder, behold Thee as my discovered inner treasure.

Thought

A birdsong concert held in spring
Delights us on our morning walk
So many tuneful songs they sing
As ears catch these – no need to talk

Conducting lead or music score
Are not required for solo trill
Rendered songs sweet and pure
The air with joy of morning fill

Now, just to be and never cease
It stays alert, moves leg and arm
Attuned to that, we feel a peace
That fills to brim, allaying harm

Prayer

Lord, you alone move all limbs and form the birds with their divine songs. Thou art the air that transmits sounds as waves the ears that catch them and the network that recognises them. I offer my joy to Thee in thankfulness and appreciation.

Thought

Blazing fires of reddish hew
Streaking through the grey of sky
Seen by creatures since the dawn
Makes us ponder why we're born?

Darkest clouds and blackest mood
Some suffering for a lack of food
We, hopeless in our helplessness
While others cry out for the dead

Relief will come as it always does
Like sun rays as they filter through
Replacing and displacing night
With artist's subtle warmth and light

Prayer

O Lord thank you for the gift of pain and suffering that contrasts with moments of brightness and joy; without these, how can I truly be inspired to look to Thee and feel Thy artistry? Grant me the gift of endurance and that knowledge that dispels darkness.

Thought

An open field where daisies grow
Feasts the eyes and feeds the soul
Under the endless blue canopy
Impressions stored as memory

In dreamy state the wakeful One
Recalls these scenes in cloudy zone
To use such scenes constructed so
Enriched by Grace in mind to flow

Illumines way on journey through
That takes me to the inner worlds
Unfolding thus this loving Grace
Beyond all dreams and sleep I rest

Prayer

O Lord by Thy Grace alone you supply thought and allow meandering attention and bring back my wandering mind to Thee. Grant that I may never lose this flow and Thy close companionship.

Thought

Subtle seeds hold secrets strange
Growth and beauty, they arrange
Silently working hour by hour
Unfolding glorious bud and flower

A part is played by sun and soil
But it's the plant that seems to toil
At Nature's pace in Her sweet time
She dresses Her forms for every clime

Perfumed scents are sent for free
A landing place for hovering bee
In gorgeous petal clothes arrayed
No entry fee for views displayed

Generous gifts for smell and sight
Allows hands to pick instead of fight
Like flowers too and their seeds inside
Share our gifts and let none be denied

Prayer

O Lord of Life, you unfold from within. I feel this with every step and breath. May I observe and appreciate your beauty and be thankful for every grace. May we share Your free gifts selflessly with others.

Thought

When we feel pinched with acute pain
Should we not merely change our lane?
When nature on paths thorns she strews
Should we not just wear toughened shoes?

When obstacles firmly stand and stay
Should we not pass another way?
To see things right and play the game
We should not use old habits same

With ease we simply shift the gears
And thus, allay all irksome fears
With lightened spirit play the sport
With Lord as partner and support

Prayer

O Lord, thank you for your loving companionship and granting me the delight of playing with you. Grant that I may always enjoy thy sport through Thy Grace and discover Thy game of hide and seek.

Thought

Why is it the sky's so blue?
An innocent asks from spirit true
"My child, it is the Lord's skin cover
He knows it is your favourite colour"

This answer from the loving Mother
Makes sky His protective cover

But others so much wiser say
That it is blue throughout the day
Because of scattered shorter waves
So, eyes from spectrum, blue it saves

But mere child am I
And He my loving sponsor
And so, I still prefer
The Mother's better answer

Prayer

O Infinite Lord fill my heart's space as your presence fills the sky. I am only your child.
May I feel the peace and security of your in-filled Love.

Thought

In slumber deep, not knowing when,
It is the time to wake.
To enter roads with monster threats
At every turn I make.

And dearly do I love those loves
That always die and fade,
Devising schemes to keep alive
The plans that I have laid.

To what avail, this drama set,
With changing mists to hide,
A golden me unformed, unframed
Awaits inside-inside.

Herein my peace above all else
Uncovered eyes to see,
With knowledge enter back to dream
Of seer, seeing me.

Prayer

O watchful Lord who safeguards me. Thank you for the pleasure of seeing You through Your misty dream. May my weariness of the world increase so Thy revelation may increase. Grant peace to every being is my heartfelt prayer.

Thought
Wandering barefoot scratched by thorn
Spirit lagging and forlorn
Fourteen years away from home
Once a king, as pilgrim roam

Love departed, threatened by lust
Re-joining her is footstep's thrust.
Gratefully found in forest hills
Strength and means to conquer ills

Assemble nature's forces strong
Forge the means to right the wrong
Fire and fury vent on that which
Stops the sacred union's kiss.

When all is done for all of man
Ayodhya's home is Sita-Ram
Back to realm and state of king.
Rejoice now and let hearts sing -
Jaya Ram, Jaya Sita, Jaya Sita-Ram!

Prayer

Lord I am estranged from Thee, wandering as I am in the midst of separation; but in special moments I see the way and thy resources always to hand. May I build a bridge to unite with thee as I conquer lust, anger and greed for thy sweet union.

DAY 20

Thought

Rippling whispering gurgling flow
In forest glades brooks babbling go
Cascading froth o'er rocky weir
Then flows on with water clear

No obstacles will stop the surge
No fallen leaves or moss will purge
With logs or boulders in the way
Streams stream on, not long to stay

Evolving nature's powerful thrust
From inside its glory must
Manifest, with trivial time delays,
More quickly so for one who prays

Prayer

O Lord may my love surge in me as it surges from thee. As water is life, so you are my life. Keep my heart pure that you may unfold yourself in me in thine own time and at thy own pace.

Thought

Where have you flown, far from home?
What new sights to eyes were shown?
Where pigeons strut on cobbled stone
Did you feast on morsels thrown?

"So odd to tell in squares I found
Empty benches on empty ground
Stepping in church and open halls
No ears there to hear my calls

With humans gone from city streets
Feeling strange with not a sound
My random thoughts took early flight
As blazing sun made colours bright

Now covered in calm silent shroud
No jarring traffic warnings loud
I felt inside away from noise
Serenity, peace, and steady poise"

Prayer

O Lord of Peace, still my mind from meaningless thoughts. Supplement my weakness by forcefully fixing my mind on Thee. May I find in the stillness that special quiet to feel Your loving embrace.

Thought

Surrounding space of infinite sky
Eagle glides with broad wingspan
Such sights make us question why
For freed state we scheme and plan

For this ideal prepared to die
Freedom's cry above all placed
Yet every step brings captive's cry
As bonds increase and threats faced

But eagle's graceful flights are made
So eagle eye can target food
Anxious for chicks from eggs laid
Restless to feed its hungry brood

If we are free but know it not
We too will hope to gain a flight
Accepting our own lockdown lot
Freedom seems beyond our sight

Full free we are and perfect soul
Our mental flights will tell us so
No need to search just play the role
Stay blissful as scenes come and go

Prayer

O Lord let me only be captive to Thee. Reveal my heart be the imprisoned splendour.
Untangle me through Thy Divine Grace that I may soar to unknown heights.

Thought

Far views of horizon broad
Of pinks and wakening hues
The calm and peace all around
And silent voice Divine was heard
Then silence broke along with dawn,
As from minarets echoes bid
Come pray – come pray this day!

Temple bells rang out aloud
And shattering shankhas fully blown
Suddenly retracing sounds
That resonate from source of OM
Come pray – come pray this day!

Church bells in deep tones did chime
To announce the hour of prayer time
Alerting pigeons flapped their wings
In praise of God and living things
Come pray – come pray this day!

I peeped in houses, huts and tents
And there I saw the simple lamps
Heard sincerely uttered chants.
And the gods were all entranced

Prayers and thoughts vibrated strong
Throughout the three grand worlds
And even in celestial realms,
The angels thronged and danced.
Rejoice, today the earth is draped
With joy and hope as new world shaped

Prayer

O Lord of constant love, I thank you for the grace of thought and prayer. I know that I have largely wasted these and yet You continue to supply Your very Self as their flow. May we all find precious time to be intensely with Thee.

Thought

In climbing steep snow bound slope
With all your effort, faith and hope
Holding fast with fearless grip
You may still slide, and you may slip

With aim to reach perfection's top
Don't think that you will ever stop
You may be lost but soon will find
Perseverance brings determined mind

Add purity, patience, and fixity of will
You will progress more, fall less until
At last, the worst of slippage breached
With grace and courage summit reached

Prayer

O Lord may Thy will be done. Grant me more perseverance, purity and patience to reach
Your welcoming arms.

Thought

One hundred years-ago today
Miraculous well stood here they say
People came from near and far
To pray for cures and fill their jar

Over entrance is a Holy shrine
Dedicated well to Queen Divine,
Who in this very place was seen
And still dwells in the sacred spring.

Now you may ask and we may tell
Where is this wondrous miracle?
Why it is here near where we dwell
We were guided here to Lady's well

Prayer

O Mother fill my mind daily only with only Thee. Thy living presence flows through my
very hands and mouth as speech; Grant only that I may discover and sip Thy waters.

Thought
"I thirst so fetch me water please"
The Lord requests on dusty trek
On village houses fronts he knocked
'Till beautiful maiden's door unlocked

Entranced and drowning in her eyes
Captured with love's sweet surprise
As time went by and wedlock sealed
He had children, cattle, house, and field

But gods of storms were then at hand
Torrential floods destroyed his land
Desperately fighting for kin and wife
Swift flowing currents took their life

Bereft of wealth, wife children, and all
He wept and shook from empty soul
Then gentle voice his depression burst
Dear, where is the water for my thirst?

Awakening there to the Lord at last
He saw that just half hour had passed
Where were the scenes of a dozen years?
And the joy that ended in sorrowful tears?

"My child", said Lord "You asked to know
What is this Maya and It's magic show?"

Prayer

O Lord of Maya, You alone can lift the veil of my delusion. Please listen to my yearning heart and out of pity for me break the spell. Grant that all may awaken from this dream world and find that peace that passes all understanding.

Thought

On Africa's dry grasslands and plains
Beasts search above for signs of rains
They yearn for days when holes were filled
They drank and splashed as water spilled

In oceans of blue that are glistening from
The dappled light plays of the father sun
Warm rays lift mists from seas and select
Pure water in gathering clouds to collect

Darkening skies around suddenly appear
Soon rumbling and tumbling drops are here
Rapturous quenching in cool nectar clean
As rivers beds fill and grasses turn green

Thought too has its cyclical dramatic play
They too get evaporated in same way
Condensing as scenery and events today
Writing script with what you think and say

Let noble sentiments and thoughts arise
Let painful ones meet their demise
Make for all blessing garland flowers
Raining on every creature loving showers

Prayer

O Lord of Mind, when selfish thoughts come to me, fill this mind with generosity and love and make it an open channel for Thy Grace to flow like a flood of goodness everywhere.

DAY 28

Thought

Choose O mind between two paths
Through forest walk of pilgrim route
One leads to kingdom unexplored
The other makes your road retraced

Remember you are God's throne room
Where ideas are formed - dispatched
Where emperor in full glory sits
Offer garlands that royalty befits

Boldly in heart's chamber tell,
Your helpful needed noble thoughts
Strong, pure, true, wise, full, and free
All these and more will come to thee

Prayer

O Divine Presence of Mind; You are easily accessible. Please remove the clutter by the radiance of Thy glory, that I may always sit with Thee in Pure Being.

Thought

Can songs of love truly tell
Of feelings inexpressible?
To capture in a verse or song
When love's madness comes along

Enduring love cannot afford
To have a motive as reward
For love is patient, love is kind
No place for selfishness to find

Pure love has pure trust no doubt
Steady when storms are about
Love knows no other rival claim
If hearts are same, none else to blame

Prayer

O Lord, all my prayers are bargaining as if you were a supply agent. You alone know my needs. You are my inner controller. Grant me only pure love for thee. Grant that I may love Thee with all my heart, soul, mind and strength, for nothing compares to Your love for me.

Thought

Who am I? Student asks one night
To one with face of wisdom's light

I am not the wind-blown mind
Nor changeful thinking intellect,
Nor fragile ego strutting proud
Nor sensitivities hushed or loud

I am He, I am He, Blessed spirit, I am He!

Not earth, nor gold nor iron nor sky
No birth, no death, no caste have I;
No status, luck or wealth have come
For father and mother have I none.

I am He, I am He, Blessed spirit, I am He!

Beyond fanciful flights, devoid of form
Permeating through living limbs of all;
Bound not by form, nor of mine or me
I fear not bondage for, I am ever free!

I am He, I am He, Blessed spirit, I am He!
(Adapted from Adi Shankaracharya's poem)

Prayer

O Immortal Self attract my mind to Thee through my Guru's grace. Grant that I may understand what Sri Shankaracharya has expressed: "if to the Guru's feet thy heart untethered still remains. Then all thou hast achieved on earth is vain, is vain, is vain."

Thought

Silky wings that kiss the air
Then folded up as if in prayer
Flirting, flitting before my eyes
Beauty displayed as butterflies

Unconscious of their magic spell
Like faery folk that legends tell
Exotic colours from artist's brush
Greet summery flowers in each bush

Nature's butterflies to me disclose
Her secret messages that She chose
Departed loved ones make it clear
I'm not gone far, I am here and near

Arising from aerial courtship dance
Larvae born from eggs on plants
From munching leaf to chrysalis weave
New self-emerge and old one leave

Reflecting on Mother Nature's play
Will chase all fears and doubts away

Prayer

O Lord, I do not thank you enough for drawing my attention to your signs and beautiful presentations. May I see Your beauty and messages posted in Your displays of love.

Thought

Cold windswept, holding firm
Midst unforgiving waters wild
Jagged rock defiant stays
Battered by the glorious waves

Strong true and challenged thus
Unmoved, calm, by word or fuss
In wind, rain and cold encased
Resolved in harshest life so faced

Without a steady cause to die
In living life to question why
What meaning is there to reply
For adversity, resilience apply

Prayer

O Lord, my steady rock, my foundation, fix my mind on Thee as thine is on me. In adversity strengthen my faith and love a thousandfold. In moments when my ego feels bruised, enter my heart in comfort that my generosity may increase.

Thought

In the beginning pure Consciousness I
Vast and without limit like formless sky
Like the infinite ocean, profoundly deep
Pure Bliss was I, like peaceful sleep

Then little wave arose and curled
Making a camp, where functions unfurled
"I am camp manager", it declared
Pride swelled in it and plans prepared

It felt separated and made a pretence
For none to prevail and break its defence
Respect was lost and compassion denied
Its urge to live was fuelled by pride

If Ego wave told its tale - how it came to be
To play wavy game with others in the sea
Knowing that a wave is still One and Divine
Many waves will come but the Ocean's sublime

Prayer

O Lord, my heart swells with joy when I feel Your being and Your play; but often times I forget and think I am separated from Thee. Please grant me the grace of constant remembrance.

Thought
First projected forceful fire
In remnants scattered, widely spread.
Some seen as impish stars to wink
At him who blinks in wonderment.

Knowledge dawns and suddenly
First light becomes reality.
From whence it came like thunderbolt?
'twas inner lamp of guiding Self.
With comrades joy and truth and love
Proclaiming silent realm profound.

Prayer
Light up my soul O Lord with that light that lights all things. May I see it in a person's eyes, in lightning and the sun and stars and as bodily heat. I thank and praise You for ever present Light. May that Light of Knowledge destroy my ignorance.

Thought

Monkeys in zoos or forests wild
Appeal to every curious child
Scratching, grabbing, playing chase
Clinging, chattering, making face

If we are careless we will find
A restless, jumping monkey mind
Aimless roaming thoughts like strays
No fixed abode and childish ways
As infants loved to play with toys
Outgrown now, they've lost their joys

So gather up the scattered things
Attention as your search light beams
Clear the way with strength of will
Take command, mind's vessel fill

With noble thoughts from every side
Settled uncluttered joys reside
No rippling trivial journeys make
Now mind is clear like glassy lake

Prayer

O Lord, by your loving grace I have turned my thoughts to Thee; while I yearn for you, in moments of childishness my attention strays. At these times, please whisper in my child ear that I, your child might turn to Thee

Thought

If we persist in asking "Why?"
We must, recall the scenes gone by.
Much more from past the mind will dwell.
Fresh causes seek - deep histories tell!

Instead, we gain from moment phase
For greatest good to now rephrase
"Why not?", "What next?", and use our skill
In contexts where we need to fill.

When, at last, true vision align
When Lord is seen as present time
And we remain attuned to Grace
Not just in time but every space

When this is so, our thanks would be
For previously suffered agony
As pains That made us to Him turn
Were means for us to live and learn

Prayer

O Lord of Time, I place myself far from Thee when I dwell on the past; in these moments I fail to see You here and now. Thank you for all the painful moments; grant me more compassion and the grace to see the milestones as evidence of Your Divine hand.

Thought

So says bard: "All the world's a stage".
Where talented thespians read from page,
Where lines are learnt, and scenes rehearsed
And actors in their roles immersed

They offer up their heart and stay
Convinced about the part they play
Now curtains drawn and taken bows
Theatre hall echoes from empty rows

Now released from make believe
Actors go home and find reprieve
From lines and painted faces go
To freely watch another show

Another drama on wide screens
Makes them laugh and cry at scenes
With actors' skills and cardboard trees
Forgetting that they're there to please

Soon, stage is blank, and worlds are none
No parts are filled, and dramas gone
And witness to these transient worlds
Stays still, surveys and gives reviews

Those knowing ones will surely tell
That only One played parts so well
The Lord with purpose, not by chance
Directed - produced the Cosmic Dance

Prayer

O Lord, Cosmic Actor. Let me always dance and sing in your creative drama. May I learn to always play my role well. Please save me from thinking that I am doing anything or profiting from actions. Grant that I may see You in the glory of Your Cosmic Play.

Thought

Sinking sun at close of day
Busy leaves dance randomly
Whisper breeze, branches sway
Flying birds are tucked away

Cool still air under quiet spell
Serves steadiness of mind to pray
Raising heart and offering flower
Heralds the evening vesper hour

Lit lamp on sacred altars stand
Chanting matches mood at hand
Day's deeds held as bouquet sweet
To lay at Lord's eternal feet

Someday our sun will go to sleep
Our boat will sink into the deep
Mourn not as your vessel lies
For we shall see a new sunrise

Prayer

O Lord, reveal Yourself to me in those auspicious times of day and night. Let me surrender my little boat completely to You as the sun yields to the beauty of evening.

Holy Mother, Sri Sarada Devi

OIL ON CANVAS 82 x 98 cms.   Artist: Pushpa Chitrak, Delhi

Thought

Who shelters you from father's wrath?
Who guides you down a thorny path?
Who nurtures, giving nature's all?
Who picks you up when you fall?

Who worries when a teen is late?
Who stands and waits at door and gate?
Who ensures good food that you ate?
Who serves with love and washes plate?

Who teaches you upon her knee?
Who shows you all there is to see?
Who listens when your heart is sore?
Who comforts you in trials you bore?

Who nursed you through a fever's fight?
Who bathed your brow throughout the night?
Who held you closer than no other?
Who can surpass the love of mother?

Prayer

O Divine Mother, I am happy to be protected and carried by Thee; who else can I turn to? Please give me the gift of gratitude and surrender, but most of all unconditional love.

DAY 40

Thought

How beautiful the bright full moon
Whose landscape gently smiles at us
She knows alone her mystic ways
Of hollows, hills and deep valleys

When dark night dome takes biting bit
Earth makes her gracious dance with it
Measured cycle comes and goes
Then round again the full moon glows

Nocturnal lamp from high up above
Reflection enchants a watery scene
Moves poet's heart and by her light
Distils mind's rays for full insight

Prayer

O Lord in rhythmic cycles, beautifully given for my eyes to bathe in. Make me purer than the pure moon. Let my mind ever rest in thee and take me by whatever path You choose.

DAY 41

Thought

City busy pulsing live
Plans embedded to survive
Arteries that deliver goods
To organic neighbourhoods

Eleven are the entrances
To this royal dwelling place
By regal presence and decree
This city runs efficiently

Unborn and like a steady flame
Lordly light inside does reign
Subtly hid from city's view
To that alone, is its life due

Control of gates bring in the best
Allow impurities not and the rest
Lord's body worshipfully maintain,
And in His throne room Him attain

Prayer

O Lord I have been careless in what I let the senses alight on, careless in disregarding Your gift of body. I see now that it is your royal city in which you live. May I ceaselessly attend to you in your royal throne room of mind.

Thought

Without love we are empty shells
That fail to take the time to hear
When listening to a tale of war
For fear of missing cricket score

Without love we are empty shells
When our eyes turn from refugees
And beatings cruel so far away
Because at home we're still okay

Without love we are empty shells
When deep sorrows raise alarms
When we don't offer bread or tea
To those who might go hungry

Without love we are empty shells
When we criticize with hurtful words
Insensitive to wounds that inflict
Because we're better and more strict

Without love we are empty shells
When we fail to shed a loving tear
When our hearts turn stony cold
While others are in slavery sold

If God is love and God is all
Can we stand aloof and be so tall?
Can't we hang on to His every word?
Listening with love to what is heard

Should not our hearts be fully bled?
When we see that He has not been fed
When He stands in pain in body mind
Can't we offer our solace and be kind?

Prayer
O Lord open up my closed heart so that there is not one grain of selfishness. Reduce my
ego to ashes and make my heart an open channel for Thy Love and Grace.

Thought

Dappled leaves and slender trees
Shy sun behind the clouds to peep
Greens and browns, flowers wild
Their scent is sent to nose beguiled

Birds with sweet and chirpy song
Seeds on lawn a breakfast throng
Air fresh cold against the face
Soles on stones feel their embrace

Arms swing and legs move on
Diaphragm piston up and down
Attention diverted from it all
Is anxious for the dollar's fall

Domestic quarrels what to do?
And all along foot moves in shoe
Oblivious to God drawing me
Eye missed the spirit in the tree

Prayer

O Lord forgive my wandering mind when you point out Your glory constantly. Grant me the faith to know that it is You who manage my affairs with Your energy. Thank You for Your spirit and Its Glory in all things.

80

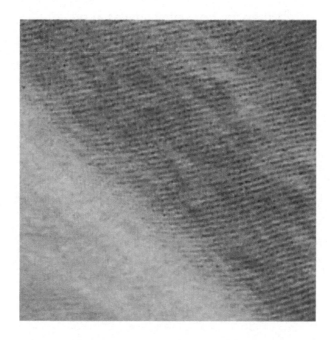

Thought

The universe like woven cloth
Is three simple strands entwined
One stretches out and one resists
And one pulls in to make it bind

Without these there would be
An immense catastrophe
They make us stay and bind us fast
So that illusive spell can last

Every child who counts to three
May learn about a trinity
And add to threefold above
God's Life, Light and nearby Love

Drifting in three worlds we glide
When in one, the others hide
Dream, deep sleep and waking time
Will make the total come to nine

Now if we stay alert and watch
When dark or selfish waves appear
And count which one of three is read
We can insert pure waves instead

Prayer

O Lord you ever hold my hand and guide me through the complex world; but I see now that You have made it simple. Let me continue to play this loving sport with Thee for as long as You want. Grant me the grace to see the blessedness of three.

Thought

Divine glory has designed
Grass in fields lush and green
Cows delight in chewing round
And flowing milk is what is found

Divine glory has designed
Streams and rivers that combine
From melted lofty mountain snows
To nourish life from their swift flows

Divine glory has designed
The wind to catch the hoisted sail
In tilting canvas man will show
He took advantage of this flow

Divine glory has designed
Ethereal waves of different kind
Where broadcasts there wait to be met
As wave flows at the radio set

When sitting in the early morn
Grace flows at your mind's front door
Don't pray for gift of grace to flow
The act of thinking makes it so

Prayer

O Lord who is pure love; You show Your love by pouring Your Grace through all things and leaving Your harmonious footprint behind. Forgive my lack of thankfulness and taking Your flowing grace for granted. May my mind be ever tuned to Thy perpetual presence.

Thought

Safe and happy were his lot
In prosperous times gone by
Now his shop was all but gone
And clothes to him did not belong

For years of work and sacrifice
Anxious debts and paper piles
Were now his mounting legacy
So, turned to God for His mercy

"Lord, money for poor I gave away
I went to church on every Sunday
Lord, save me now in my tottery
Let me win the national lottery!"

Many weeks and months he prayed
And on his knees for hours he stayed
Then shaking fist through teary mist
Burst out - "God you just don't exist"

Then clouds dramatically rolled away
God's booming voice was heard to say
" My child, this wish, for you to get it
At least please buy a lottery ticket"

Prayer

O Lord increase my faith in You a thousandfold in Thy nature and myself; may I post my intentions without wavering doubt and be Thy simple trusting child again.

Thought

Gazing into flames at night
Sparks fly off to left and right
Leaping spears, the gods unseat
Radiate energy and their heat

Fragrant grains and yellow ghee
Rounded fruits and sweet honey
Chanted mantras every spoon
Auspicious for the phase of moon

Burning furnace is my heart
Glowing rays reach every part
Smelted turmoil feelings fused
To golden love for all confused

Prayer

O Lord Thou art the fire, the lightning, the inner warmth and blazing sun. Thou art the inner light in the deep recess of the heart. Grant that I may ever feel Thy radiance and warmth and share Thy radiance as an open channel of Thy Grace.

Thought

Visits from old friends for tea
Companions of a childish me
But now, I can new friends invite
Resist evil not, or enemies fight

Four Rs in sequence can be tried
With diligence used and applied
React, review, revalue, reframe
Is how to play with life as game

First impression, "please do come
Let me review where you rose from"
See it from the Lord's throne view
Revalued makes reactions new.

Rehearsing this for habits changed
Shaped best reactions rearranged
Old friends are asked to go away
New lingering ones allowed to stay

Prayer

Lord – forgive me Thy foolish child who wastes the use of the gifts of precious moments.
Grant that I may, in the now, play this loving game with Thee of replacing the old
playmates with the new.

Thought

Is earth a source not a resource?
Does a bird fly or ride the wind?
Does a fish swim or is it carried?
Do flowers flourish from within?

Think on these and listen, listen!

Do you digest noon day food?
Do you apply the cooking heat?
Do you or water quench a fire?
Do you have the heart to pump?

Think on these and listen, listen!

Do you or body change in time?
Do you recall or scenes supplied?
Do you replace the worn-out cells?
Do you breathe or lungs inflate?
Think on these and listen, listen!

Prayer

O Lord, my ego has for so long assumed agency, but it is You who do everything without demanding return, or thanks. You do this because You have a purpose in mind. Lord I humbly offer Your gifts back to You with tears and thanks

Thought

Did you know how great is He?
Who spins suns in the galaxy
His wealth is such a vast amount
For I take charge of God's account

His real estate beyond all measure
Celestial realms a hidden treasure
In ledgers I've listed His qualities
Compared to Him no one exceeds

But I've not met this king of kings
Only counted His assets and things
Not sat with Him exchanging looks
For what I know is just from books

Wiser ones entering sacred door
His royal presence to explore
Know the light of all things lit
So will not arrange a divine audit

Prayer

O Lord! let me not keep a distance from you by counting up Thy glories, but only open Thy door when I knock and keep me with You – You just gazing on me lovingly and me gazing on Thy face of love.

Thought

On tilted axis spinning sphere
Lessons from advancing year
Unwrap the gifts from almanac
For free trips round the zodiac

Memories of childhood thrills
How we developed special skills
Equipped to face all obstacles
That push us round again in circles

Folded palms prostration thanks
For filling up our memory banks
Selecting those that urge us on
We re-arrange till pain is gone

Our vision composes destiny
From music, dance and imagery
Creative moves as dream presents
New shapes of people, and events

Prayer

O Lord Most times I forget the good fortune given freely to me. Thanks, seems hardly adequate and I know you don't require it, but my love for you does. "Lord open my lips that they may sing your praise" in a continuous song of gratitude that you are here, are now and are love.

Thought

Mirror, mirror on the wall
Am I stout, fair, thin or tall
If I change my style of hair?
Or the fashion clothes I wear?
Will this improve an image me?
Enhance possession bodily?

I, bound by mine so limited
Haunting me in muddled head
Dogged thus by darkness clung
That thwarts real air of freedom
Try as I might to resist and shake
Ego's stronger the more I wake

Combat, curse and chase away
Will not keep "I" shadow at bay
Boldly walk toward sun's face
Shadow behind at leisurely pace
Free of ideas of "I" and "mine"
Free soul lives for humankind

Prayer

O! Lord! Grant that I may learn to see these shadows for what they are in the shadow world and trustingly turn my face to Thee as flowers turn their face to the sun. Let me not resist evil but look on Thee alone.

Thought

A noble prince was born this day
Foretold by an auspicious dream
The garden in which he came to be
Was symbol of his luxury
His future greatness as a king
Was challenged by his destiny
Flaws removed or screened away
And every ill was kept at bay

Every wish was his to make
Three palaces for him to take
Fine princess in a contest won
And they had a fine young son
Ready to rule beyond the gates
Channa bring fine chariot drawn!
Four told things they could not hide
Sickness, old age, death outside

Why does this man look so strange?

Bodies suffer because they change
Why is this toothless man so bent?
His youthfulness has all been spent
Where do they take this sleeping man?
Death comes to all, we know not when
Who is beggar with keen sharp look?
Searching for truth and life forsook

Resolving strong the truth to find
He left his palace life behind
Farewell to dear ones lying there
In forest soon cut off his hair
No compass, map or scripture read
Eschewing tortuous austerities
He found compassionate middle way
In which mind can in calmness stay

On just one hand four fingers tell
That suffering can be managed well
Eight fingers held will simply say
Change the direction, here's the way

Prayer
O Lord Gautama Siddhartha who came blazing forth as the Enlightened One. Grant us
Your simplicity and compassion

Thought

A nut, a fruit some milk and bread
Consumed happily with prayer said
Transformed to body benefit reaps
While waking ego dreams and sleeps

Enthroned lord by will and skill
As angels dressed to serve him fill
They make all bodies minds as field
Where His plans become revealed

Limbs, heart and surging thought
Reveal his love where flow is brought
Gifts graciously accepted, undeserved
To attain the heights for you reserved

Prayer

O Lord cure my impatience; grant that I may catch Your grace in the present moment, to welcome Your plans and new blessings. Grant that I may keep my mind on Thee and be ever absorbed in Thee.

Thought

Coloured glass split light collect
Flickering lamps shadows reflect
Walls with carvings etched inlaid
These sacred spaces man has made

Stone solstice solid giants stand
Distant spires on highest land
Lift soaring mind to noble heights
Inspiring us to rapturous flights

For years on end on sacred soil
For God's glory, workers toil
Their skills applied for no reward
Creating space to praise the Lord

Curved arches, domes, calligraphy
In timber, glass, and masonry
Leaf of gold and marble walls
Decorate pillars in temple halls

Pilgrims from far look up in awe
And gaze around to see much more
From hands and muscles, lofty dreams
Came sanctuaries under timber beams

Prayer

O Lord, thank you for manifesting Your energy in so many wonderful ways. May I be content to be Your willing and uncomplaining instrument for Your glory and through this to inspire others.

Thought

Battered boats, roof tops fly
Circling vortex winds pass by
Not that sins have made it so
For good or bad, high and low
It is only Nature's way

Staring out as droplets fly
Pangs give rise to teary eye
There will be no friends today
Virus lockdown so they say
It is only Nature's way

In lonely moments young or old
Laments can come if past is told
Melancholic tales of "poorly me"
Unless balanced with some sanity
It is only Nature's way

Those who offer roof and food
Without a thought for gratitude
Attentive listening on the phone
To those abandoned and alone
It is only Nature's way

In their sharing and compassion
Find their humble sharing ration
Is privilege rare for them reserved
Beloved One can now be served
For it too is Nature's way

Prayer
O Lord in moments of self-pity, show me how you are suffering; my heart is full of sorrow on the one hand and joy at your presence on the other. I fully offer without reservation these limbs for thy service with no pause to idly think of my own suffering.

Thought
As sun sinks down at evening time
Mood subdues as church bells chime
Red orb round earth waves ritually
Bright lamps and prayers held faithfully

Divine life rays and solar mass
Is made from swirling twirling gas
Furnace heat fused from its core
Urges man to worship more

Spinning planets roundly praise
One who makes their lengthy days
Ancient seers' minds were bright
Sought to find who lights this light?

Prayer
O Lord I have taken it for granted that you have arranged things rhythmically out of play
and love. I adore you and thank you for your face as the sun.

Thought

One day death will knock on door
One day heart will beat no more
One day breath will slow and rest
One day death will come as guest

Be sure last thought you make
Is one of give and not of take
Know each second marching by
Is last moment's last supply

These unused series learn to fill
With purity, truth and love until
Mind is soaked in nectar sweet
Flowing from Lord's sacred feet

Every night beyond the dream
Events to happy peace will yield
The sleeper then does not respond
In dress rehearsal for beyond

Prayer

O sweet Lord of peace and rest far from the ocean's roar. Displace all selfish thoughts that I may saturate the mind with Thee.

Thought
To see Lord sit within is thrill
His penetrating fullness fill
And then to know that all is He
Transcending this discovery.

Children who are taught to pray
Think this Lord is far away
Fingers point to cloudy sky
"They say he's there, but very shy"

At colleges where chins are stroked
Debates, discussions are provoked
Students agree - consenting nod
Impossible whereabouts of god

Playful Lord of hide and seek
Asks where am I? You cannot peek
In all live I as inner guide
You can't see from the outside

You failed to grasp me like the air
But that's because I'm everywhere
Don't put me in a fixed domain
For upon myself I play this game

Prayer

My pure delight O Lord is to catch the at thy play. In moments of doubt when my attention wanders, let me always see thy face in and through and as and beyond.

Thought
Friend sat breathless pale
To relate his woeful tale
"Pounced upon was I on road
Vicious blows on me bestowed.

Dark enemies like robber band
Quickly gained the upper hand!"
"For justice sake name these brutes
So I can make them face law suits"

Objects on which senses alight
Some on heavenly gains delight
Assaulted souls on stormy seas
Forget these cravings are enemies

Raise self-up and steer aright
Attention as friend for to fight
Armed strong with learnt abilities
Conquer all these enemies

Prayer

O Lord, when things go well, I neglect Thee and when they go badly, I blame Thee. I am my best friend and my worst enemy; but You are my only constant companion.

Thought

Trust that Mother Nature fill
The gaps She would supply
Watchful of a stall and still
As rippling streams flow by

For hands to open and accept
Free gifts that life will show
Cling not to hoardings kept
But release and let them go

Faith in teacher, self and God
Will bring a peace of mind
Underfoot the paths you trod
Have all been left behind

Prayer

O Lord I trust in You; remove all remnant doubts and fears that surface under stress.
Your loving hand is always outstretched to me. I let go, release and trustingly allow You
to carry me wherever you will.

Thought

Warm white sand below my feet
Running through my toes
Winds pick up grains that meet
Ocean's fragrance enters nose

Standing squishy shifting sand
Shapely shells arrive beneath
As foamy cooling waters land
Fresh offerings to me bequeath

Pausing for each sense to feel
Inside a surging sigh of awe
Before horizon's freedom kneel
As spirit's waves arise and soar

Swimming diving like a fish
Splashing playing like a child
Floating calm with thankful wish
For my playmate God has smiled

Prayer

O Lord, it is only you that brings unspeakable joy; there is nowhere that You are not. I have drunk Your cup of bliss. May we all fill our cup to overflowing with Thy transforming love.

Thought

Glistening snow-capped crests,
Floating on a clear blue sky
Standing there from ancient day
What sacred teachings you convey?

Sharp crystal air refreshing face
Messages from Vedic race
Noble heights stay far beyond
The things of which we are fond

To meditate on peaks pure white
Yogis' minds gain deep insight
Fixed like mountain seated still
Gaining strength, resolve and will

These, not just cold and solid blocks
Or pushed up heaving icy rocks
Great Lord of Yoga seated there
With indrawn eyes and flowing hair

The earth itself he made His seat
Meadows, foothills for His feet
His tresses long are valleys steep
So snow can thaw to rivers deep

Prayer

O Lord uplift my mind and hold me there in Thy highest realms. Make our thoughts
noble and lofty. May my inner tranquility beam thy glory to every being just like You as
the grand and beautiful Himalayan mountains.

Thought

Suddenly dark moody cloud
Can come from memory store
Grip of fear leaves us cowed
Distress shakes us to the core

Brooding on the pain from past
Unsteadies mind and nerves
Illness will take hold at last
Draining off our last reserves

But simple remedy can apply
Our caring mother told us how
In place of heaving heavy sigh
Ask the mother soothe the brow

I have a mother tell yourself
Whenever you are in distress
Thus will you restore the health
Without a need to convalesce

Both the wicked and the good
Are her children close and dear
So when cut or bruised you should
Allow her to remove your fear

Prayer

O Mother, in times of distress and hopelessness I forget that I have a mother. Thank you for reminding me so many times when unasked you rescue me. As soon as I feel your motherly consoling arms I feel happy.

Thought

Let us go to island place
Awkward troubles never face
Enjoy warm tropical breeze
Amidst palms and azure seas

The tragic things on BBC
Escape the stress and never see
Nothing there to spoil our view
Or argue with those that we knew

New fights arise in paradise
With insect stings pay the price
From own self, is no escape
Carried on subconscious tape

Hurricanes can blow away
The very island where you stay
Floods destroy a little house
And soon escape plan will douse

Unless mind is well attuned
To blissful base below the wound
Where you are matters not
Unhappiness came when you forgot

True paradise is all around
When presence in all things is found
Feeling inner rapturous joy
Happiness will unhappiness destroy

Prayer
O Divine Presence, bestow your abundant grace on me and all that I may always feel
you be it day or night and with every breath that comes from thee I offer back to thee.

Thought
Best teachers change our painful life
That in the home of husband/wife
Dwell with respect and loving ties
By showing way as moods arise

When spirit swims in deeper life
In spirit partners can unite
Adoring oneness in each other
Even more than sister brother

Offering each half their whole
Entwines eternally in one soul
With special bond together bind
To be best teachers for mankind

Prayer
O Lord, it is not sufficient to merely see You in each other, may I deeply feel you in every man and woman and lovingly offer you the fruits of our closeness by humbly serving You not only in temples made of bricks and mortar but in those made of flesh and blood.

Thought

Finding faults in rocky hills
Is part of every climber's skills
Viewing flaws of man at worst
The seer's mind's polluted first

Abrasion gathers pain and hurt
Leaves mind dry and desolate
Through it mind becomes enslaved
And makes it even more depraved

Forgiveness is for soul unbinding
If peace you seek, stop fault finding
Eye splinter seen, correcting flaws
Is blurred by grainy tree in yours

Treating thus whole world as kin
Easily removes the stain of sin
Golden goodness found in man
Rejoices at His glorious plan

Prayer

O Lord, there are times when I selfishly don't share myself with others; times when my mind and speech are critical of Thy children. I know that when I am open hearted your divine grace flows. May this be my constant state.

Thought

As philosophers are wont to do
Heated arguments construe
Objections, dialectics, pros, cons
Formlessness or formed icons

Wise mystic saint had this to say
In guiding seekers on the way
Heady gymnastics made to please
Are like explorers counting leaves

Averse to taste of numbering speech
Some will want to further reach
Seeking something far more sweet
Their delight to juicy mangoes eat

Golden yellow pulp and juice
Stained mouth used as slurping sluice
To watch a child's delightful feast
In wide eyed wonder joy released

Prayer

O Lord when your precious gift of thought is wasted on analysing and counting and playing trivial pursuit, my heart closes and I no longer feel your presence. Open up my heart to you alone so that my speech may be only of thee and I may taste the sweetness of your flowing love.

Thought

Strange but perfect shining clouds
Reflecting light rays from the sun
Creating tents in awesome crowds
Reminding me of where I run
Resorting to my homely soul
Whose radiant light makes all things whole.

Contrasted with a rainy sky
Your golden edges only seen
Like delicate maiden coy and shy
Behind a latticed nature screen
And then in playful mood enthrall
As veil moves on-revealing all.

Prayer

O Lord of Beauty. Thank you for the glory of your maya-surprises that lead my mind inwards unexpectedly. I am often overwhelmed by these moments that You choose for me. May I always respond to your loving call.

Thought

In slumber deep, not knowing when,
It is the time to wake.
To enter roads with monster threats
At every turn I make;

And dearly do I love those loves
That always die and fade,
Devising schemes to keep alive
The plans that I have laid.

To what avail, this drama set,
With changing mists to hide,
A golden me unformed, unframed
Awaits inside-inside;

Herein my peace above all else
Uncovered eyes to see,
With knowledge enter back to dream
Of seer, seeing me.

Prayer

O Lord, witness of all, presiding over all my worlds and states, emotional, creative and potential. I am yours; you are mine and I am thee.

Thought

Busy we can learn to be
Like a buzzing honey bee
Gold black stripe flash in flight
Flower blossoms yield the right
To collect pollen nectar sweet
As hazy wings don't miss a beat

To work indeed we have the right
Not to complain, protest or fight
But if we store up things beware
Wax cells and honey we prepare
Will be robbed from active hive
For others to eat to stay alive

Be not alarmed or bring out stings
Our privilege's to share our things
And bee of mind can choose to sit
On best of flowers nectar sip
We can from edge drink honey bliss
Or blissfully swim below surface

Prayer

O Blissful Lord may my life energy be ever dedicated to Thee; may my mind be selected on what it dwells on; may it ever be immersed in your bliss not that I alone may enjoy it, but that I may share this nectar feast with others.

Thought

It is not in misery but in joy
That we ascend a mountain path
Drinking in with eyes recalls
Displays of ferns and waterfalls

Trekking up a winding way
No angst but pleasant panting breath
No thought for what a journey brings
Just to walk while wild wind sings

Grand distant hills lord over lakes
Mirrored in the waters clear
Calmed still mind reflects the same
Like artist's scene in picture frame

If life's a journey, enjoy your stay
Plan not for tomorrow but today
Though at the top vast vista waits
Unhurried steps enchant mind states

Prayer

O Lord cure my impatience. Thou are here, thou art now and thou art beauty. Replace my anxiety for results with the awareness of each delightful step on the journey.

Thought

Notes that good musicians play
I too can master this one day
When selected instrument is right
Practice must be day and night

Put aside all doubt and fear
Tune the strings to please the ear
Accept mistakes as tutorship
Correct each one with ownership

Faith in self will slowly grow
Patience when progress is slow
When love of music I possess
I've gained a freedom to express

These steps to liberation take
Steady progress you will make
Fear now conquered, sure and free
Means I can play each melody

Prayer

O Lord you guide my faltering steps; you are my divine helmsman. Taking me by the hand you take me to the point when I can let go and freely play with infinite joy the sweet music of life divine.

Thought

Western isle remote and green
Sacred land of harp and song
Dotted sheep on hills in fields
Tales of gods and Fionn MacCumhaill

Saints and scholars were not weak
Their Celtic blood was fiercest streak
Their words struck hearts of lesser men
Their shining lives, their art and pen

Noble stock announced new dawn
A Brigid in Tyrone was born
Power, strength and virtue hold
As in the missionary days of old

Race toughened by Atlantic wind
Resolve that cold could not rescind
Burning flame of zeal for cause
Revolutions over oppressive laws

Each soul Divine should mankind know
In Éire this message too should go
Inspired by Irish heart and blood
From here this news the world will flood

Hearken all with Om as bell
That rings out true at Ladyswell !!

Prayer

O Divine Helmsman; your grace has flowed in your own time at your own pace in the sacred pilgrimage area of Our Lady's well. Your inspiration on the one side was matched by your response on the other. Blessed art thou.

Thought

Ancient man discovered fire
Worshipping it fulfilled desire
Embers to cook, kept spirits high
In rains and cold they kept him dry

Now far away from sheltering caves
After mastering the winds and waves
Tides and gravity were enslaved
For trade and travel roads were paved

After this, shall harness for God
Powerfully shifting flames of love
For history's second time transpire
Man will again discover fire

Prayer

O Lord I discover only what you reveal. Please stoke the burning flames of love in me until my heart bursts with fiery passion and spreads to all mankind so that it may smelt us all in golden oneness.

Thought

Windy currents ruffling hair
Breath of God to purge the air
Fresh infilling blowing sails
As directed wind prevails

White sea horses ride on top
Currents wild stir ocean's pot
Dark rainy puffy clouds collide
Seagulls above enjoy the ride

Is weather good or is it bad?
Discussions on this can be had
Mind when lifted up like wings
Sees only what its Mother brings

Prayer

O Divine beyond virtue and vice, good or bad, positive or negative, love or hate, sweep
me up in Thy rapturous arms that I may joyously glide in the currents of your love.

Thought

If our father we ask for bread
Will he give us stone instead?
If his kingdom is heart's space
Will we not there see his face?

If we repeat his holy name
Will he not be there again?
If his kingdom's all around
Will his glory not be found?

If childish will be put aside
Does his willing grace abide?
If he provides our daily need
Will we worry who will feed?

If fatherly care sustains today
Will we feel he's far away?
If he forgives our infant ways
Will we forgive our enemies?

If eyes he hides in peekaboo
Can he not open them for you?

Prayer

O Fatherly Lord, whenever I fall you pick me up and carry me without my even knowing.
May I feel your strength and guidance from moment to moment and understand my
origin and inheritance from Thee.

DAY 78

Thought

I dreamt that I was high in flight
The sea on left the cliffs on right
I felt swift angels lent me wings
So I could do inspiring things

Light as feather on the breeze
Floating free with gliding ease
Voice heard "go forth my child"
Be destined for the Emerald Isle

When everywhere the signs say "Go"
Don't hesitate with movement slow
Divine urge impels inner man
Clears paths ahead for greater plan

Prayer

O Lord, when my will is done it results in hurt and pain; but when my will aligns with yours, I see how things unfold easily. May I listen more intensely to your voice of wisdom over my foolish protests.

Thought

The Word descended once again
In response to mankind's pain
Before It said "This one but sleeps"
Flesh form arose and life it keeps

It spoke "Let ancient land arise"
Remember wisdom of the wise
In fifty years that land awoke,
Slavery chains snapped and broke

Word is stirred, descends for one
Who calls on It when ritual's done
In loving company prayer kept
Even when most sleepers slept

Holy words best company
When mind requires good remedy
When robber twins attack their prey
Protecting thoughts stand in the way

Prayer

O Lord, you are on call twenty four hours of day and night; from age to age you come; but when I call your name, you are immediately present. Lord, let my diligence increase and may thy sacred name be ever on my lips.

Thought

Slots of time in units come
We shouldn't waste a single one
Precious seconds used to worry
Are wasted time to make us sorry

Remember that today's the tomorrow
Of yesterday's worry that you borrow
Thoughts make trillions of cells excite
With what you think, wrong or right

So have not pastimes that are filled
With past times making cells not thrilled
Creative thoughts from fresh mind work
So Lord's body functions like clockwork

Prayer

O Lord, I offer this body and mind for your exclusive Divine purpose and use. Since it is yours alone and you are its inner controller, I fully trust in Thee and offer it wholly to Thee in all thy seconds provided.

DAY 81

Thought

From noisy streets and market place
Turn longing gaze to see thy face
Where praising angels chant and tend
To king of body citadel

In shapes of living and of still
Inside and out does fullness fill.
While intent makes a pliant mould
To house the royal king's household.

Like air that freely carries sounds
The Self within/without abounds.

Prayer

O Lord inside and pervading all, despite your loving gaze on me and my distracted
attention pitched elsewhere; through your loving grace and out of compassion for me
reveal your fullness that makes fearlessness and freedom our own.

Thought

Beyond imagination universe vast
Grasping frame we stand aghast
Whirling spirals, spin like tiny dots
On canvas black, countless shiny spots
Nearest disc reached in thirty billion years
And by that time maybe it disappears

Senses only catch scenes scattered wide
The greater truth beyond blind spots will hide
Those who know totality and secret of it all
Will see the space of intervals as skin of overall
Cosmic body of great Lord to opened eye will see
That the sparkling jewels above are Lord's accessory

A thousand arms, a thousand eyes, a thousand legs and heads
Looks to us like filaments of luminous heavenly threads
Quantum leaps of joy as vision cleared like dawning days
Divine parts are playing parts in seeming vast arrays

Prayer

O Lord, in my small exchanges of love with Thee, my ignorance blinds me to your overwhelming totality; yet in your chosen moments of grace, you give me, your helpless child, a glimpse of your grandeur to elevate my soul. Grant me this from time to time when my mind lags behind and gets dragged down.

Thought

Chariot of sol is soul of earth
Drinking rays, life has its birth
Facing it, our sphere's pole tips
Stretching day before sun dips

Earth's tilt at twenty three point four
Brings festivals from solstice lore
To praise sun's zenith in the sky
Some hoisted giant stones up high

Life giver worshiped earnestly
Illumines mind with vibrancy
Saluting sun with graceful moves
Strength of mind and health improves

Prayer

O Lord who shines in my depths like the rays of the sun. You give me life, yet I wrongly attribute everything to me. I meditate on your glory that has produced this life and this universe; may you enlighten our minds and inspire our understanding.

Thought
Not for food or fear I leap
But frolic in the spray I sweep
Splashing writhing acrobat
Blissful state my habitat

In ocean of pure ecstasy
My soul is swimming joyfully
Jumping joy uncoiled in me
Fish out of water is still free

No fisher net or worldly lair
Can catch me sailing through the air
My energy soars much higher than
Mere body of a mortal man

Prayer
O Lord, you are always here, but when my attention is pitched elsewhere it brings pain. May your energy not be wasted but gathered and offered back to thee in an upward surge of joy. Praise and thanks to thee as your joy unfolds in me.

Thought

Wide awake when people meet
Poor, deprived or rich elite
Gain or loss their action brings
As causal realm pulls in those things

Like space around rose flower beds
In subtle waves its fragrance spreads
So cosmic beams unfailing mould
Beneath the thoughts as scenes unfold

Five senses deal with elements
Formed or mixed ingredients
We add or change to suit our need
In ways that make our lives succeed

But when constituents are free
From perceptions and their quality
They work beyond sense boundary
As pure waves in their primacy

Prayer

O graceful Lord, thou art all the world and beyond. Thou art the ocean and the waves and the three states of consciousness. My vision is only the crest of a crest of a wave. Grant me your divine vision to see and feel your creative force.

Thought

Thoughts with aim and purpose yield
As they go forth in mental field
Tanmatras move to coincide
Mix and shape the world outside

Wisdom, strength and grace divine
If these we seek for all to shine
That grace as wave foundations laid
Must bring unceasing unasked aid

Discords are angels sent to tell
"With holy thoughts fill mental well"
When this is done pure waves get urge
To take soul to Divine Truth's verge

Prayer

O graceful Lord, thou art all the world and beyond. Let me merge my mind in Thee and so better shape the world for the welfare of every being. May all beings be brought to the verge so that nearness becomes oneness.

Thought

Whispers wandering across a sky
Like sundry thoughts floating by
Fond memories and wistful sighs
Covering truth that dream belies

Solid world of rocks and stones
Aims and goals and golden thrones
For a few minutes will bemuse
Till death arrives and these we lose

The lord of death said please behold
Of wealth and land to you be told
Offers for which men strive so hard
Discerning ones will soon discard

Faith and sense demands to know
What tempting offers fail to show
That steady one that changes not
When whispery wanderings forgot

Prayer

O Lord, many temptations and desires beset the mind, instead of squandering your gift of time with these, let me embrace your gift of discernment that dissolves them quickly. I lovingly accept your gifts of faith, hope and love that dispel cravings and selfishness.

Swami Purnananda is the Spiritual Director and Founder of the Ramakrishna Centre in Dublin Ireland (Éire Vedanta Society nee). He was initiated into spiritual life by Swami Vireswaranandaji Maharaj (a direct disciple of Holy Mother) and for many years, he underwent spiritual discipline and studies under the direction and tutelage of Swami Nihsreyasanandaji Maharaj (a direct disciple of Swami Shivanandaji Maharaj) whom he served as his Personal Attendant and Secretary and from whom he took his monastic vows in 1981. In 1992, Swami Purnananda was elected President of the United Cultural Institute in Zimbabwe, where among other things he established an educational bursary fund for deprived girl students, a feeding programme for the poor and he also continued the work of spreading the message of Vedanta in Southern Africa. In 2006, he was invited to Ireland where he has been preaching the converging truth of Vedanta since, as Spiritual Director of the Vedanta Society which he founded. Well versed in Vedanta, Yoga, Comparative Theology, Psychology and Science, the Swami conducts workshops on Personality Development, Spirituality, Meditation, Yoga, etc. as well as guiding and counselling others. Swami Purnananda has contributed significantly to the Interfaith movement in Ireland. He dedicates his life to assisting and guiding others physically, psychologically, and spiritually. He has expertise in psychology and counselling, and he has assisted individuals and groups in many aspects of their lives including enhanced health through applied naturopathic principles. Additionally, the Swami has contributed towards important international scientific research in the use of micro-organisms in mineral processing. An engaging speaker and writer of many articles, the Swami also pens poetry and paints.

More about Éire Vedanta Society: https://www.rkmireland.org/

Printed in Great Britain
by Amazon

32244828R00086